Praise for
DO I DREAM OR WAKE?

DeWitt Henry's flowing, essay-like poems allow for sur-
prising convergences and divergences as they probe their
subject matter, which is as varied as a house-to-house search in
Watertown, Mass, after the marathon bombing; a kaleidoscopic
view of Henry's roles as husband, father, brother-in-law, and
grandfather; and an account of a serious physical setback and
the resulting medical intervention and later healing. **The
poems synthesize literary touchstones--including MACBETH,
THE MERCHANT OF VENICE, ROMEO AND JULIET,
and HAMLET--with the spectrum of lived experience. Each
is a voyage; our travel is guided by the poet's ability to
think deeply about who we are in relation to others and to
ourselves.**

Jennifer Barber
Author of THE SLIDING BOAT OUR BODIES MADE

What pleasures are to be found in these extended med-
itations! **Each narrative is wise, witty, and learned.** As in
the most compelling autobiographies, **DO I Dream OR Wake?**
transcends its genre. This captivating array of situations and
circumstances transforms the personal into the universal.
Open it anywhere and discover yourself!

John Skoyles
Author of YES AND NO

FIRST EDITION, DECEMBER 2024
ISBN 978-1-953136-91-6 HARDBACK
ISBN 978-1-965784-07-5 PAPERBACK

Cover Graphic Design & Book Typography by Kurt Lovelace.
Cover photography by DeWitt Henry
Cover type *Bauhaus Dessau* **Alfarn** by Céline Hurka,
Elia Preuss, Flavia Zimbardi,
Hidetaka Yamasaki, and Luca Pellegrini.
Author name, blurbs, footers in **Jenson** by Robert Slimbach.
Back cover description in **Gill Sans Nova**.
Titles and body text set in **Baskerville**.
Flourishes set in Emigre Foundry **Dalliance** by Frank Heine.
Emigre Foundry **ZeitGuys** by Bob Aufuldish, Eric Donelan.
Typefaces licensed Adobe, Linotype, Emigre, & URW GmbH.

PSPRESS.PUB
PIERIAN SPRINGS PRESS, INC
30 N GOULD ST, STE 25398
SHERIDAN, WYOMING 82801-6317

TO MY
GRANDDAUGHTERS

EVA

MAYA

OLIVIA

CONTENTS

Do I Dream or Wake?

ON CULTURE

1

High, low, middlebrow.
Advanced, primitive;
Dominant, sub.
Exotic, familiar.
Religious, political,
multi-, counter-,
pop, consumer.

Wars, clashes, shocks;
appropriations.

When in Rome…
Celibates in Paris.
Pork lovers in Tel Aviv.
Big Macs in New Delhi.
Marxists in malls.
Feminists in mosques.

Cultivated suggests
charm school grads,
well-trained and mannerly;
sharing social values.

Also plowed, seeded and
watered as in farming
and gardening.
From Latin cultus
for care and adore.

Sperm and egg, or virus
in a petri dish.

2

As social conditions worsen
and mainstream religions fail,
we grow acculturated
to cults, argues Amanda Montell
(in *Cultish: The Language
of Fanaticism*).

False prophets seek profits
and power as cynically
as Dostoyevski's
Grand Inquisitor, who
talks shop with the true Jesus
before executing him
as a heretic.

Some worst examples:
Jim Jones convinces
nine hundred followers
to commit "revolutionary suicide"
in Jonestown, Guyana (1978).

Marshall Applewhite
convinces thirty-eight members
of Heaven's Gate to follow
his passage from earthly life to
"a next level" via UFO (1997).

My writer friend, Jerald Walker,
grew up in Herbert W. Armstrong's
Church and Co-Workers

With Christ, "a white supremacist
doomsday cult." described by
by 60 Minutes in 1979
as an $80 million fraud.

Walker's parents both were blind
and sacrificed to pay tithes
while raising their six children.
A "Great Tribulation" was imminent,
yet as Church members, Jesus
would save them, restore their sight,
and fly them to paradise in Petra, Jordan.

Armstrong also preached that
his was God's only true church.
"All others were the devil's,
especially Catholicism."

When Walker first heard of
the Peoples Temple suicides,
he could "definitely imagine
Mr. Armstrong ordering us
to take our lives when the end-time
prophecies failed. And
we would have done it....
Many of his followers
still would,...including
half my family."

3

Occulture stresses
secret powers, magic,
and the paranormal—
think Voodoo, Santeria,
Wicca, and spirit mediums—
while Satanism profanes
Christianity and Judaism:
"Better to rule in hell than serve
in heaven." An FBI probe
in the 1990s found no
actual Satanists performing
human sacrifices or
ritually abusing children,
despite a national "Satanic Panic"
and 12,000 accusations.

Hawthorne's "Goodman Brown"
meets "Rosemary's Baby."

4

And what to make
of ISIS? Medieval doctrine
applied to Millennial despair.
Cultivated terrorism.
Crusade for Caliphate.
Innocents murdered.
Women oppressed
by marriage and rape.
Suicide bombers promised
harems in heaven.
Media masters.
Psychopath martyrs.
Chop logic and muddle.
Cultural heritage sites
and artifacts destroyed.

5

From age 14, Jerald Walker
left cult for anarchy:
street gangs and drugs,
until a friend was murdered.
Then turned to education,
found a writing teacher
in community college
who helped him attend
the Iowa Writers Workshop.
Went on to marry,
have children, and
publish his memoirs;
became a professor
and administrator,
cultivating others.

6

Here is an American note,
struck by Matthew McKnight
while reconsidering Albert Murray's
Omni-Americans (1970):

"It is said that choosing
  not to identify as black is selfish,
  or a betrayal, or an evasion of history—
  despite the universal promises
  such a position holds.
  At its best and most sincere, however,
 'transcending race' doesn't mean
  ignoring its history or the force
  it has on the lives of people
  all over the world,
  but [does mean] walking and talking
  in terms of an idiom
  with universal applicability—
  what keeps in mind the suffering
  that all people face...."

7

James Alan McPherson
(following Murray
and mentoring Walker),
put the American challenge
this way: "if one can experience
[America's] diversity,
touch a variety of its people,
laugh at its craziness, distill
wisdom from its tragedies,
and attempt to synthesize
all this inside oneself…
one will have earned the right
to call oneself a citizen
of the United States."

8

My culture is American,
with all its virtues, faults,
and contradictions.

As for Global, two
cheers for the Humanities,
"The best that has been
thought and said,"
but how do we agree on best?
Our spirits moved? Time-tried?
Consensus overruling
difference and doubt?

Conditioned to science, tech,
media, drugs, and -isms,
perhaps we need
more reason to relate.

"Train all to be fair and kind,"
reads my artist daughter's tag
on the abandoned tarmac, once
a parking lot for Raytheon workers,
who made Patriot missiles.

SHOFAR

A ram's horn (or antelope's),
naturally twisted from base
to pointed tip; then bone and flesh
are hollowed out.
Bell at thickest, mouth at tip.

Why a ram, the novice
children ask (or don't)?

Because Abraham sacrificed
a ram in place of Isaac?
Because God's chosen
were nomad shepherds?

My first was an astonishment.
Long as a trombone.

At home, with our
young daughter, we balanced
simple rituals, Hanukah
and Christmas, Passover
and Easter; and Connie's
Friday night Shabbat candles.

Now Connie had befriended
a conservative couple
and their daughter who lived
down the street in our
blue-collar, mostly Catholic
Boston suburb, where we
scraped by on grants
and part-time teaching.

Invited to their Rosh Hashanah dinner,
I felt alien and polite,
while Arnie, the husband,
pedantically performed
prayers and rituals
that even Connie
must have found forced.

Just before we sat to eat,
he lifted a lengthy, twisted
animal horn out of nowhere,
opened his front door and blew
a series of loud blasts,
like a semi's air-horn;
then slammed the door.

No explanation. Ludicrous,
I thought, stifling
a laugh. Through the doorway
I'd seen the shock
of a passerby, an elderly woman
stopped in her tracks.

🌿 🌿 🌿

Connie had grown up in Miami,
compared to suburban
Philadelphia for me.
Her father had been troubled,
then divorced; and died
while we were dating.

Her mother was her hero,
bringing up and putting
four children through college,
while working as an accountant
and trying to write musicals.
Her family impressed me
as more spiritual than
religious; more permissive
than pious, as was my own
as lapsed Presbyterians.

Before we were married,
I met an uncle of Connie's
who warned us about
mixed marriages: you're neither
one thing nor the other.

But no one else opposed us,
not even Connie's older brother, Dan,
who had been a debate champ
at B.U., attended a yeshiva
in Brooklyn, then continued
studies in Israel, where he worked
on a kibbutz, met Lauren,
and was ordained as a rabbi.

We traveled to their wedding
in Chicago. Lauren's father
was a wealthy showbiz exec,
and friend of Frank Sinatra.

Dan was hired by
a conservative congregation
in the suburbs near Skokie.
With help from Lauren's father,
and from Sinatra himself
(who asked Dan for spiritual advice),
he raised money to build a synagogue,
and grew in reputation and career.

From a distance, Dan and I
practiced mutual regard,
but I also felt defensive.

Jewish law proclaims
a child of a Jewish mother
to be Jewish, regardless
of the father's lineage,
however Connie celebrated
our "both-ness," and we
raised our children without
official religious instruction.
Otherwise, once grown,
let them each choose.

❧ ❧ ❧

Dan had five children with Lauren:
Sara, Ari, Rena, Elan, and Avi.
With Ruth at 11, and our son
David at 4, we gathered again
for Ari's bat mitzvah, a service
in Dan's new synagogue,

filled with congregants, men
on one side with yarmulkes
and prayer shawls, women
on the other with scarves.
There was a lectern in front
and behind it, the ark,
which Dan opened, lifted out
the synagogue's Torah scrolls
and spread them on the lectern
for Ari to read aloud in Hebrew
and discuss his chosen passage.

Clearly Dan was highly regarded
as a spiritual leader and citizen.
He was learned and intense.
He spoke and sang with a
penetrating baritone; and was
handsome, groomed, and affable.

They lived nearby in a new
split-level, many-bedroom house,
with a pool in back. Lauren
was warm and beautiful
and always felt close to Connie.
The cousins enjoyed cousins.

After this first formal service,
I attended others over
the years with Connie:
bar and bat mitzvahs

of friends', and other cousins'
comings of age. I knew what
to expect and how to behave.
Many Passovers and Rosh Hashanahs,
her younger brother Ray's wedding,
with Dan presiding.
The arbor and Chuppah,
the crushed glass, the dancing
and lifting bride and groom
overhead in chairs. Our daughter's
on public beach near Cartagena,
with Ray presiding because
Dan couldn't make it. Shivas.
Recitations of the Kaddish.
My only funeral, for Connie's Mom,
who died in New York from cancer
(whose body had been prepared,
according to precise rituals
by her children under Dan's direction,
then shipped to Miami for burial
beside her mother). "Don't step
on graves," I was directed.

   ✿   ✿   ✿

After our children were grown
and raising families themselves,
we grew closer to Dan.

He'd come on reverses
and hard times.

He'd divorced Lauren and
resigned from his Chicago
congregation; then overseen
a prominent synagogue
in Miami. Professionally,
it seemed a step up. He felt
welcomed back by the city
he'd grown up in, and
where his elder sister,
Lonne, lived. But after
a few years, he lost the post.

Then, diagnosed with
bladder cancer, he'd undergone
a radical cystectomy.

He lived in pain and spent
half of each day (he said)
on hygiene. He struggled
to change medical bags.

He lived in a run-down
apartment complex
north of Miami. Lonne
helped him with rent.
He kept a car. He shopped
for himself in a kosher market.
He couldn't manage money.
He had social security,
and medicare, but no savings,
and only occasional requests
to officiate at ceremonies.

Connie worried about his
isolation, despair, and
suicidal thoughts.

She called regularly,
listened to his lectures
and opinions, shared
childhood memories.

Partly (I thought)
to please him, she chose
to practice their religion more.
Our daughter followed her lead,
as did her daughter. Together
they studied for a
triple bat mitzvah,
with a trans rabbi,
where Dan visited, spoke,
and gave his blessing.

We visited him as well,
the both of us, or Connie alone
and to comfort Lonne now too,
who in the midst of Dan's ordeal,
had developed multiple myeloma,
and underwent three years
of clinical trials
before she passed.

Later, we visited Larry,
her husband, alone in Miami,
and shared in Lonne's aura.

Dan drove from his apartment
to join us and he and I
rehearsed our rapport.

He asked about Shakespeare,
about fate in *Romeo and Juliet.*
Was this justice? Innocents
sacrificed by a greater power
to punish their parents?

"Yes, for hate bred from airy words,"
I said, "and prejudice. But also more
complexly, each young lover
had choices— not as worldly
as Anthony and Cleo later on,
but still confused
and blessed by dreams."

He frowned, "Dreams?"

"Eros and bliss," I replied. "Spirit
in flesh. 'Eternity was in our lips
and eyes.' Felix culpa."

(Was he thinking of his own
parenting or mine? Had he read
my memoirs and poems,
which Connie had had me send?)

In turn, I asked about
the meaning of shofars—
and he seemed happy to explain.

Shofars were sounded
to awaken souls, especially
on Rosh Hashanah, the new year,
when believers examine their deeds
and seek atonement; and Yom Kippur,
ten days later, when God's judgment is sealed.
"As the horn takes in breath at one end
and sends out the other," he suggested,
"So God replaces Judgement with Mercy,
and blessings for the coming year."

There were four ritual blasts,
he added, always to be blown in order:
a long, single blast;
three short wail-like blasts;
nine staccato blasts of alarm;
and a great long final blast
for as long as you can.

He could show me tomorrow.
Our return flight was early.
And he'd be glad to drive us
at six a.m.; no need for Uber.

Our luggage in trunk,
he wanted me in front
and Connie in back, but as
I moved to get in, there was
a curled, polished ram's horn
in my seat. It was maybe
eight inches from bell
to curve, then straight up

another eight up to the tip.
Its grain was cream on tan,
smooth, and shiny.

I got in and held it,
thinking it was for show:
the Rabbi's personal shofar.
But Dan said it was his gift
for me. Except I'd have to
to learn the blasts and he'd
test me later on the phone.

As he drove, he explained.
"You purse your lips for
a farting sound, except no
tongue." I tried, just air.
He took and held it with
his right hand as he drove.
Our windows were down
and he sped through
a round-about. He blew
his "blaaaat!" out his
window, louder than car horns.
"Okay, you try." Handed it back.
I puckered up like a trumpeter
and puffed, surprised by
a rich, full-throated, "blaaaat!"
"He got it, I think he got it,"
Dan sang from *My Fair Lady*.

At home I was irreverent,
tooting to amuse; but also

practicing. For Shabbat,
we face-timed Dan with
our daughter and granddaughters.
Dimmed the lights.
I blew my Shofar sequence,
loving its brief wailing cries
more than alarums or triumph.

Two years later, Dan's phone
wouldn't answer for days.
Ray flew down to check,
and with police and medics
broke open his door and
rushed him to the hospital,
conscious, but too late to save.
He died two nights later.

Connie (vaxed, boosted, and tested
for Covid), flew down alone
to clean out his apartment and help
with the shiva and funeral.

I followed the graveside service
on zoom. Connie, Ray , Larry,
Elan and Ari (two of Dan's sons)
and one close Rabbi-friend spoke,
praising Dan's religious nature,
his learning, his help to
countless congregants, and
his leadership in interfaith work.

"Life had held rough waters for you,"
  Connie eulogized, "but you loved
  the ocean in all its glory. While
  aching at things lost, your pride
  was with your children."

"You know," I remembered him
  confiding while depressed,
"I still believe in God.
  I've never doubted my faith."

✻ ✻ ✻

I keep the shofar on my desk.
From time to time, I raise
and sound it to his memory.

Do I Dream or Wake?

Eroticism? Spirit of flesh?
Religion of touch?
What is figure, what ground?,
What is substantial,
and what dream?
Are dreams prophecy,
miracle, or self-delusion?

The "affirmation" in
Romeo and Juliet
is poetry itself. They
are teens, of course,
idealistic compared
to their corrupt elders.

The lovers' imaginations
are as literal as anything
we take to represent
the play world.

"More light," demands
  Juliet's father at his feast,
  meaning more torches,
  more literal light
  on the day-lit stage,
  where for story's sake
  we allow for night.

"Oh, she doth teach
  the torches to burn bright,"

marvels Romeo, as if
at supernatural luminescence,
which neither the audience
nor other characters can see.

☙ ☙ ☙

We might agree with Juliet
(at first) that Romeo's metaphors
are more hackneyed than inspired.

She dismisses his vows
by the moon, "the inconstant moon,"
then literary vows altogether.
"Well, do not swear."
He has her love. If honorable,
just tell her where, when, and how
they can be married.

☙ ☙ ☙

With help from Juliet's
bawdy nurse, the friar
secretly marries them in his cell,
hoping that their alliance
will end their families' strife.
Meanwhile, we know from
the opening prologue
that only their deaths
can accomplish that.

Literal deaths appear
with Tybalt's (Juliet's cousin)
slaying Mercutio (Romeo's friend).
Romeo, enraged, slays Tybalt,
which results in the Prince's
banishing Romeo from Verona
on threat of execution.

Before he leaves,
the nurse helps to smuggle
Romeo into Juliet's bed
for their wedding night,
And their parting at dawn
is crossed by dread of
never meeting again.

☙ ☙ ☙

Juliet threatens suicide
if forced to marry Paris
(the Prince's kinsman),
and to commit secret bigamy.
So the Friar offers a potion,
distilled from flowers, which
will put her into a death-like
coma. Her body will be left
in her family's crypt next to Tybalt's.
Meantime, he'll tell Romeo
to sneak back for her awakening
so they can escape together.

However, the friar fails to allow
for news of her death reaching Romeo
before the friar's messenger can.

※ ※ ※

Romeo in Mantua wakes
from a happy dream, where
he was dead, but then, revived
by Juliet's kiss, becomes an emperor.

On hearing of Juliet's death,
he never questions cause,
e.g. the plague, say, or as
a suicide from missing him.
but embraces his worst fear.
Defies fate; buys real poison,
and rushes to join her.

※ ※ ※

In the tomb, Romeo
mistakes signs of Juliet's
reviving as added
reason for despair.

Reality is bitter, willed,
and ironic. This vault is
a "feasting presence,
full of light," recalling
their first meeting,

Juliet is a beacon. Her
cheeks are ruddy, not ashen,
as if death is now his rival,
"and for fear of that"
he will join her forever,
and "shake the yoke of
inauspicious stars"
from flesh itself: eyes,
arms, and lips. With that,
in anguish, he runs
his ship on rocks. Drinks
his poison as a bitter toast,
and even with a dying kiss,
forsakes their reunion.

❧ ❧ ❧

Juliet awakens to the terrified
friar. Sees Romeo dead,
kisses his lips in hopes
of tasting poison—"Thy lips
are warm!"—and realizes everything.
Their love. How close they came.
His desperation in believing
her dead. She takes his dagger,
calls it "happy," meaning both
lucky and glad, and stabs
herself (becoming its "sheath").
We can't question her conviction.

※ ※ ※

Ah, felix culpa! The lovers
embody paradox, merging
contraries: reality and dream,
light and dark, medicine and poison,
bitter and sweet, bedroom and tomb,
fate and free will.

While Christian doctrine
condemns love suicides
(see Dante's seventh circle),
here they serve divine ends.

"All are punished.".
  Rival households reconcile.
  Montague will erect a
  golden statue to "true
  and faithful Juliet," and
  not to be outdone
  Capulet will pay for
  Romeo's, lying beside her.

Yet Verona's future seems sterile.
No youth remain except
Rosaline and Benvolio.
Dawn remains "glooming."

※ ※ ※

Has performance mended
"What here shall miss"?

Are we helped by promise
of the friar's earlier sermon
("what is [nature's] burying grave,
that is her womb")?

Do we blame fate and parents?

Do we dismiss the play as fiction,
agreeing with Mercutio
that dreams "are children
of an idle brain, / Begot
of nothing but vain fantasy"?

And/or do we allow that stage
deaths have no sting?
That boy players rise
in person for applause;
their characters revived
for each next performance.

(The consolations of
Midsummer's Pyramus and Thisbe.)

Even as I indulge
transformative wonders—
the mutual passion of as-ifs—
glorifications, miraculous kisses,
immortality, incandescence,
grace and bliss;

I like to imagine
Hamlet as the author,
a skeptical philosopher
who broods about his
mother's infidelity,
vengeance for a murdered father
and his own love for Ophelia.

Fuller and more perplexing
tragedies will follow.

ALL BUSINESS

Is it the tragedy of Shylock
(who is gifted, victimized,
and flawed)?
Or of Antonio
(whose love for his
protege is sublimated
by the protege's
marriage to an heiress)?

Or the comedy of Portia?
(who teaches
her lover the danger
of conflicting loyalties;
and who traps Shylock
with his own legalism).

Is this a play about love
and prejudice? Or
a prejudiced play?

No doubt Shylock
in Elizabethan times
would be taken, at first,
as a stock villain, e.g.
Marlowe's Barabas, or
the deformed Richard III.

Given Anglican persecution
of both Jews and Catholics,
is the play protesting
religious intolerance in the name
of common humanity?

Was W.S. defending himself
as a recusant Catholic,
money lender, and bi-sexual?

Is the Muslim prince, Morocco,
among Portia's suitors,
rejected for his race
as well as his religion?
(His boast that his blood
is reddest prefigures Shylock's cry:
"If you prick us, do we not bleed?")

Both widowed fathers fail
to know what's best for daughters—
first, the Belmont tycoon, who
distrusts Portia's judgment
and relies on his will and riddles
to expose fortune-hunters and fools;
while Shylock tries to lock up
Jessica in his "sober household."

Portia calls herself
"an unlessoned girl"
and grants indigent Bassanio
control of her inheritance and self,
so long as he never gives away
or loses his wedding ring.
He vows he never will.,
unless he's dead.

Rom-com crosses with tragedy.
Antonio has agreed to Shylock's
terms for Bassanio's loan
with a pound of his own
"fair flesh" for surety,
a condition so absurd
as to seem only figurative.
Shylock calls it a "merry sport."

We know from an aside,
however, that Shylock hopes
"to catch" Antonio "on the hip"
and hates him as a Christian,
one who rails against his usury,
lends out money gratis,
and hates the Jewish nation.

Still Shylock only turns
murderous once betrayed
by Jessica, who elopes
with a Christian,
and steals his money and
his one sentimental possession.
her dead mother's ring,
which she trades for a monkey.

He blames the Christians,
rather than his parenting.
They've perverted flesh
of his flesh, haven't they?

Turned her against him.
Jessica is as dead to him
as if murdered. He seeks
an eye for an eye, blood
for blood. though no one
has been killed yet,
(except, perhaps,
in pogroms elsewhere).

No sooner engaged,
than Bassanio hears from
Antonio, whose argosies
have sunk. He's failed
to repay Shylock on time.
Now Shylock seeks his life.

Portia intervenes;
puts off their honeymoon,
sends money with Bassanio
to ransom this "dear friend."

Secretly, she's ready
with an instant solution;
sends to her cousin,
a judge, who arms her
with a legal loophole against
Shylock's loophole, plus
garments to cross-dress
as his law clerk and
letters authorizing her
to decide the verdict.

Shylock has studied law
enough to expose Christian
hypocrisy ("among you,
many have slaves…"),
but still not closely enough.

Portia argues for mercy,
offering both principal
and profit; but Shylock's
hatred is compulsive.
He stands here "for the law."

Antonio braces for martyrdom,
as Portia grants Shylock
his pound of flesh,
yet by the letter of the bond
"no jot of blood." If Shylock
draws blood or fails
to cut exactly one true
pound, his lands and goods
will be confiscated.

"Is that the law?" Shylock gasps,
at once aware of his hubris.

There is still more, as Portia
and the Venetians pile it on.
His punishment, under a law
against any alien's attempt
on a citizen's life, is for
half his wealth to go to Antonio,

the rest to the state, and
only the Duke can pardon his life,
which the Duke does. But then
Antonio adds a coup de gras.

He will invest Shylock's money
in trust for Jessica and Lorenzo,
while granting interest to Shylock;
but only on condition that Shylock
convert at once to Christianity.
The Duke revises his previous
pardon to depend on this condition.

Shylock, a broken man, is "content,"
choosing survival over martyrdom.

Venetian Catholics might
have viewed forced conversion
as merciful, but believers
in religious freedom don't.
And W.S.? We'll never know.

The play goes on to explore
the balance between literal vows
and honest, realistic ones
(similar to Act V in MSND).

Portia, still in drag, is
surprised by Antonio's shaming
Bassanio into giving his ring
to the "clerk" in gratitude.

She returns first to Belmont.
where Jessica and Lorenzo
as caretakers mock
their religious differences;
resumes her identity;
plans "merry" revenge.
as a teaching moment.

Bassanio arrives,
triumphant with Antonio;
but when asked for the ring,
is forced to admit that
he's broken his bond,
albeit for Antonio's sake.

In response, she threatens
to "ne're come in your bed
until I see the ring."
But Antonio intercedes,
offering his "soul upon the forfeit"
should Bassanio break faith again.

She agrees and gives Antonio
a new ring for Bassanio to "keep…
better than he did the other."
Of course, Bassanio recognizes it
and she admits: "For by this ring,
the [clerk] lay with me."

She hasn't betrayed Bassanio,
however, since she herself
had been Balthazar, the clerk.
Then adds news that Antonio's
argosies have come to harbor.
Antonio is speechless.

Bassanio goes on to joke
about the fear of infidelities:
the clerk shall be his bedfellow,
who can sleep with Portia
whenever he is gone.

The shadows of Shylock,
of Antonio's loneliness,
of possible betrayals,
of religious and tribal hypocrisies,
of literal conditions,
and of women patronized:
all are held in abeyance
if not exorcised.

And Belmont is more rarefied
than Venice, worldly marketplace.

COMMUNITY POLICING

In 2007, Chief Edward Deveau
told our meeting of
The Citizen's Police Academy
several stories about
emergency calls on 911.

As a writer, I had signed up
to learn more about
Watertown, our multi-ethnic,
blue-collar suburb
west of Boston, where
I'd settled after grad school,
raised a family, and
commuted to my tenured
teaching job downtown.

I was bookish. Most
of Watertown was not,
nor was its police force.

Deveau himself, I guessed,
was French-Canadian,
where our dominant neighborhoods
were Italian, Irish, and Armenian,
mainly white, Catholic and
Greek Orthodox. Each group
had its civic club. Each sought
to preserve its home country's
heritage and language.

He seemed cultured,
intelligent, tall and slender,
though his voice was flat
and diction slangy.
I'd read about his past.

Born and bred in town,
he'd played basketball
for Watertown High; attended
Westfield State University;
worked as a security guard
and private investigator.
Began with WPD in 1983
as a night patrolman.
Promoted to Sergeant in 1989,
then Lieutenant in 1992.
He attended the FBI's
National Academy in '99;
was promoted to Captain;
became Chief in '01.
He was married with
no children.

He told us one story
about domestic violence;
played the scratchy recording
of the call for help.

A woman's voice, frantic:
"My father's shooting my mother!"
Dispatcher told her calm down;
what address? "10 Oak Street...
He has a gun, he's outside her car.
It's a blue Nissan." What's your name?
"I see the gun!" Is it little or big?
"My brother..." Officers are there.

They'd found the Mom in the car,
shot a number of times.
The father had fled.

Officers gave her first aid.
She'd locked herself in,
and the husband had shot
through windshield and window.
A miracle she was alive.

Deveau had investigated.
The issue was divorce.
They were a traditional family
and the father couldn't understand
how the wife had been awarded the house.
They had three children. One daughter
was getting ready for college. The son
had confronted the father and
they'd fought; and the father
had driven away.

Deveau met the son and daughters
when he visited the Mom
in the hospital some eleven times.
He wanted to calm them as victims.
A special memory for him
was the Mom telling her daughter,
"I want to see the day
you get married."

A few hours after the shooting,
they had caught the father.
A Medford trooper had spotted
the car, and at gun point
arrested the man, who was eating
a donut, and had a .38 revolver
beside him on the floor.

The case went to trial.
The mother recovered and testified,
but forbid her kids to testify,
too traumatic. Father was charged
with attempted murder, which carried
a twenty year sentence, but lawyers
argued for five with a guilty plea.
The mother testified that
she would live in fear and the judge
gave him ten years. Devastated,
the man died in prison after four.

Deveau saw the mother
soon after he'd made Captain,
and she'd told him: "My daughter,
she got married…I lived to see that!"

His story ended on that line,
and his eyes glistened.

I looked up the case
in our town newspapers
(on microfiche in our library),
dating from Spring 1995.

The father had been
Madiros Mancelikilj, aged 65;
and the mother, Sima, 50.

They'd emigrated to Watertown
from Istanbul in the late 1970s,
after the birth of their third child.

They'd been counseled
for "marital problems" by
their Armenian Church Pastor
for twelve years before the shooting,

The Pastor said they both spoke Turkish
and couldn't find a professional
who did; hence "fell through
the cracks in the system."

Sima was the primary wage earner.
Madiros "contributed no support
to the family." In 1986,
he had threatened Sima
and police had taken him away.
In 1993, he had hit her head
with a lead pipe. They had
taken out restraining orders
against each other, and both
had sued for divorce. He wanted
money from their house,
worth maybe $500,000.

❧ ❧ ❧

Deveau's big moment
proved to be the shootout
with the Marathon Bombers
on April 19, 2013. He led
state police, federal agencies,
and surrounding communities'
officers in a 20-hour search
for Dzhokhar Tsarnaev.
He locked down Watertown
while swat teams
searched door to door.

Finally a resident reported signs
of life in his boat, which was
parked in his backyard.
They captured the boy alive.

Deveau's media presence
showed star quality.
He was lucky "to have
carried out a mission
that I had never trained for,"
he told interviewers; he also
emphasized that the capture
had been a team effort.

State Senator Ed Markey
took him to Obama's State of the Union.

He announced his early retirement
in 2015. He was writing a book,
and in demand as a speaker.

He remarried as well,
to a woman who owned
a Boston bakery.
They moved to Back Bay and
made the society pages.

His most vocal critic remained
a recently retired woman

councilor, and a career contrarian—
who offered to help my own wife's
run for a council seat.

She told us that Deveau had been
the Manager's ally
in a group of insiders
who profited from selling out
the town to developers.

They'd worked to destroy
the councilor's reputation,
surveilling and serving her
with tickets for petty offenses.

And, she confided,
"This kind of man…I know
he used to beat his first wife,
before they divorced."

ON MIGRATION

To *e*-migrate from homeland
is to *im*-migrate to new,
and settle, put down roots;
and Watertown, my adopted town,
west of Boston on the Charles,
prides itself on layered heritages.

Irish immigrants fled famine, Italians
poverty and war, Armenians genocide:
many were attracted here to industrial jobs at
Watertown Armory (munitions, atomic and otherwise),
Hood Rubber (sneakers, boots, and tires),
and Raytheon (radar, microwaves and Patriot missiles),
but even earlier the river-powered mills for paper.
for clocks, and for the Stanley Steamer.

As industries failed, children *em-igrated.*
Population fell from 50 to 30 thousand
by 1976, when Connie and I arrived from Cambridge.
We rented from a first-generation Italian family.
The live-in landlord and his wife
only knew a little English
and we had to guess each other's meanings.

Michele (Mike) was a contract plumber.
His cousin next door, taught science
at the middle school.
On the other side was Guisseppe,
a mailman. In back was a vegetable garden.

Connie and I had each first im-migrated
for colleges (BU, Harvard),
leaving families in Miami and Philly burbs.
We courted, and married.
In Cambridge/Brighton our apartments
had been filled with students from everywhere,
headed for anywhere with new degrees.

We'd left the singles world of Harvard Square,
intent on starting a family, and
Watertown was about families—
religious, settled, working class.

We'd agreed to no pets,
but when our landlord heard
that we were expecting,
he hesitated. "Bambino?" Later I overhead
his wife, Dorinda, pleading
(seemingly) our case in Italian.
Our daughter was born. And
we stayed there eight more years.

❧ ❧ ❧

By then we both had teaching jobs
as well as my mother's inheritance.
We bought a three-bedroom Cape
in a neighborhood half a mile
away and two blocks from the river.

We adopted our infant son
from Seoul, Korea, and raised
him with our daughter.

❧ ❧ ❧

Each MLK Day, Watertown
celebrates diversity with an annual breakfast
where 400 attend. Prizes for high school essays
are awarded; a diversity speaker delivers the keynote.
Restaurants donate hot food. Chorale groups sing.
Pols glad-hand. It strikes me as
our town's best spirit forward.

❧ ❧ ❧

Worst, by contrast, was intimidation
by a teen gang and its leader
on the block where *Ploughshares*,
the literary magazine that I had
co-founded, moved in 1977 from our
apartment into a run-down storefront.

A fire station adjoined the block in back.
Facing the street were a laundromat,
an Irish bar, a pizzeria, a karate studio,
then us, a newspaper distribution drop,
a general market and an auto supply store.

Each store had plate glass windows,
where the morning sun bleached wares.
Ours had a front room, like a fishbowl,
then one long room behind it, which
was blocked from street view,
except through the full-length
glass of the front door. Six hundred
square feet first floor, plus
six hundred in the basement,
it once had been a barber shop;
most recently a display room
for novelty lighting fixtures.
Rent began at $300.

The landlord was the grocer,
Eddy Kardejian and his wife Marie,
who had inherited both the market and
properties from Eddy's father.
Both had kindly, open personalties,
as did Paul Sullivan, the pizzeria's
owner and cook, who attracted kids,
barflies, firemen, and local residents.

I never knew the gang leader's name.
He lived around the corner in
a trailer-sized two-bedroom
owned by his mother,
who lived with a fireman.

He sat with buddies across the street
on the gas station's curb

and threw rotten apples that
splattered on our window.
He shouted at my coming and going,
"Hey, hey! Library fairy!"

(I remember my older brothers'
story from back in our
Philly suburb, how, during
World War 2, they had
tormented a laundry man,
banging his storefront window
to get a rise and shouting
"Chinky, chinky Chinaman!"
so he'd rush out cursing in Chinese
and chase them with a bat.)

I didn't want to engage.
I worried we'd get a brick
through the uninsured window.
Our screen door did get slashed
and its bottom plate kicked in.

Husband, father, writer,
editor, and teacher, here I was founding
a literary magazine on a shoestring,
grants, and volunteerism. By day
I lugged in bags of mail from
a PO box in Cambridge. Or
crammed my car with canvas
mailbags sorted for non-profit mailing.

Three times each year, an eighteen-wheeler
managed to back in behind the storefronts
and wheeze to a stop. We'd unload a skid
of twenty-some hundred-pound boxes,
and trip after trip, wheel them inside.

To these neighborhood kids,
their parents, and to guys in the bar
our "business" made no sense.
How could we manage rent?
We had a stream of volunteers
and interns, mostly young women.

My first Managing Editor, Joyce Peseroff,
drove from Arlington for three days
each week. Readers for fiction and poetry
signed out submissions and returned keepers,
then signed out more. Guest editors
visited for manuscripts and stayed for lunch.

Many nights I had the office
to myself to work on my novel,
read, or grade papers. I hung
black-out blankets at the entrance
so no light showed. I heard voices:
"Anybody in there?" "Naw."

Kids liked to loiter under our
overhang, to smoke, finish a slice,
drink beer, or shelter from weather.
"Ploughshares? Fuck is it?"

"Dunno. Library books or something."
I heard the splatter sound.

Since the backdoor only
locked from inside, I waited
for them to get bored and leave.
I felt that if I suddenly stepped out,
asked them to move, and locked
the front door behind me,
I'd be asking for more trouble.

One night Pizza Roma was set
on fire. Kids had broken in
Paul's back door, made hamburgers,
and left his grill on. In our
storefront, smoke stained every surface.
Pick up a manuscript and its exact
shape remained like a shadow.
The smell lingered for weeks.

Eventually, the gang leader
got his license, joined the Navy maybe;
in any case, he disappeared.

We became a fixture for fifteen years,
financed by state and federal
grants, fundraisers, and by
Emerson College, where I taught
full-time and chaired the Writing
Department. We turned our fishbowl
into a borrowing library. Computers

and a dot matrix printer replaced typewriters,
filing cabinets, and files of 3x5 cards for addresses.
Our first calculator simplified bookkeeping.
The College stored admissions brochures
in our basement. The karate studio
was replaced by a catering service.

We agreed to move our operations to campus
and formalize our Emerson affiliation,
but still kept the storefront for storage,
at least until fifty-five back issues
had been digitalized, making it pointless
to store more than a few cartons.

By then, Don Lee, my tech-savvy
former MFA student, while serving
as Managing and Associate Fiction Editor,
joined me in the melancholy task
of carrying 55 cartons of pristine,
unsold back issues up the basement stairs
and dumping them with display stands
(recycled from the town library)
my desk and chairs and other off-street
furnishings along with trash bags filled
with papers and other books into the bed
of a trash removal truck.

I dropped off my keys to Eddy, the landlord,
who was confined to his home nearby
with an aggressive cancer. Marie let me in.
He was watching TV in pajamas

and arguing with his elderly
mother-in-law, but was glad to see me.
He'd been fond of Connie, and
always given treats to my son
(I also gave him each new
Ploughshares issue, which Marie enjoyed).
They were selling the block to a developer.
He missed the store and his friends.
I wished him well and shook his hand.

ON HUMANITY

Not all humans are humane, not even saints,
best selves; or any of us all the time.

When the woman oiler on Kurosawa's
Runaway Train calls her male companion,
the escaped convict, an animal, he counters:
"No! I'm worse than animal. I'm human."

A priest-principal in Brian Moore's *Feast
of Lupercal* warns a virginal teacher
about romance with a young female protestant:
"All men are human. But that's no reason
to show we tolerate it."

Less than divine or super- (though better
than sub-), ancient Greeks envisioned gods
with human shapes and passions. Shakespeare's

fairies mock each other for presumption:
"Lord, what fools these mortals be." Drugged,
Titania falls for Bottom. We congratulate

ourselves on being compassionate, bi-ped,
featherless, smart, and fashioned
in the image of our creator—however
varied in gender, race, IQs, strengths
and weaknesses—and doomed to die, unless
we reproduce first; live on in legacies
and genes.

❦ ❦ ❦

Hamlet saw us as unique; splendid
or meaningless according to our choices,
fates, & grace.

❦ ❦ ❦

Harold Bloom credits W.S. with "inventing
the human" by exploring personality,
psyche, conscience, and inner-life.

Contrary to Aristotle's rule that
a tragic hero can never be a villain,
we're immersed in Macbeth's temptations,
raptures, terrors, visions, insomnia,
and passion-clouded wit. At least until
he has children murdered; loses his wife
to madness; feels only nothingness; sees
his life as a tale "told by an idiot,"
dies fighting MacDuff, a grieving man ("My
children too?") whose victory sets time free.

❦ ❦ ❦

Age eight, I'm with my mother in Woolworth's.
I see a bin of mail openers shaped like
M1 carbines with bayonets; smitten,
I have to have one; but Mom says no
and moves on. I linger, pick one up, check

to see if anyone's watching, shove it
in my pocket and follow her through
the check-out. Back home, I either show it
to her, or she sees me with it and knows.
She tells me this is wrong. We have to go
back, confess, return it, and apologize.
The manager, a lesser power than father,
goes along with my important lessons:
Thou Must Not Steal. Honesty is the Best
Policy. I am shamed and forgiven.

❧ ❧ ❧

Apes are "humanoid." Give or take a missing
link, we're also naked apes according to
60's zoologist Desmond Morris. Ask Coco.

❧ ❧ ❧

Radio announcer at Hindenburg
disaster: "Ah, the humanity!"

Neil Armstrong on moon: "One small step
for man, one giant leap for mankind."

❧ ❧ ❧

18th century philosophies called
human rights "inalienable": life,

liberty, and the pursuit of happiness.
The U.N.'s 1948 *Declaration*
added: food, shelter, clean air, health,
education, and practice of religion.
Human dignity is "Something you
somehow haven't to deserve." It belongs
to all of us equally, although one group
may degrade, enslave, and dehumanize
another.

🌿 🌿 🌿

Forget the art in a burning house, save
the human being.

🌿 🌿 🌿

I cautioned my teen-aged daughter not to lose
herself in social causes, since she admired
our closest family friends, who were activists

for peace. "You do what you can, and live
with what you can't," I told her (I did!). I

even cited the passage from *Middlemarch*
about the "roar" of tragedies "on the other
side of silence," and how it would overwhelm
us, unless we wore ear-muffs like airline
baggage handlers. Fortunately, she didn't

listen—to me. Or if she did, argued
back over years to come with her dedicated,
gifted life…

※ ※ ※

From Third World Studies at Hampshire
to a semester in Guatemala;
travels to Europe, the Middle East; a Fulbright
to Bogata, Colombia; hip hop writer
and singer; painter; single mom; part-time
ESL teacher in Chinatown; tending
bar at Wally's Jazz Club; youth arts
director at Jernandez Cultural
Center; she started hip hop exchanges
between Boston and Cartegena youth;
worked for Partners of the Americas;
moved to Cartegena with her daughter
(then four); met and married Diego, who
shared her vision; embraced *The Gospel
of Hip Hop* by KRS-One as her guide;
had a second daughter; moved back near us;
taught Spanish full-time in Middle School;
earned her MFA in Public Art; became
instructor in "Kingian Nonviolence
Conflict Reconciliation." Was supported
by her Principal and town officials
in moving our suburb towards a "Beloved
Community," until a right-wing blogger

blamed her for indoctrinating students
with woke-prop about the history of policing.
Our local cops felt betrayed in the midst
of budget hearings. An anonymous
caller made threats. Super of Schools decided
not to fire, but put a warning in her file
for failing to ask parents' permission. After
taking personal leave, she chose to resign
instead, risks working as a full-time artist.

"Art is one of the strongest bridges
I know," her website reads; "winding us between
and across enemy lines, smudging borders
like so much charcoal dust."

Commissions, grants, and sales have been enough
to provide for life and family without
teaching. They live just up the street.

꧁ ꧁ ꧁

In materialistic nations, charitable
tithes are a decency tax, while actual
taxes buy health care, education, public
safety, sanitation, communication,
roads, bridges, disaster relief, the myriad
machinery of modern life. Religious
nations are fanatical. Their faithful
masses endure want, while believing
in a paradisal afterlife.

In all nations, perhaps, the ignorant
and powerless endure the non-mercy
of the propertied, ruthless, the best armed.

Brutal or kind? Gated communities?
Security? Border policy? Miasmas

of language. Of society. Of culture. Of
resources. In a cattle car to doom,
only the fittest survive. Or luckiest.

Or think they do.

❧ ❧ ❧

Our man-made probes seek extra-terrestrial
life but have revealed only barren worlds,
so far. Only matter. Not even microbes.

While in human anatomy, with other
probes and tools, with chemicals and surgery,
we treat our cancers and our infertilities;
repair or replace vitals (some with
transplants from donors; others
made of artificial parts). Bomb cells
with radiation. Devise miracle
drugs for pain, for emotions, for new viruses.
Splice DNA to kill genetic disease. Map
the circuits running our brains. Only, still
we've never found the seat of soul.

THE KINDNESS OF
STRANGERS

Trip as in journey, or as in drug,
or as in stumble, say, like the scholar
who falls into a ditch while stargazing
(an outworn parable, even for Chaucer).

※　※　※

Eager for my book-fair signing
that convention morning, I breezed through
the hotel lobby. Running shoes, jacket and cap,
computer case with books over my shoulder.

Scanning the lobby, spotted no friends,
kept on through the revolving door, down steps. 2. 3.
past doorman, past strangers with convention badges.
Down to the street lane marked with orange
and beveled for the handicapped, I thought.

I'd walk the mile to the convention hall.
Looked for cars, stepped out to cross, was
falling, tripped, jarred off balance by
the unexpected curb drop (no bevel!);
twisted to take the blow on my right side.

Memories of bike accidents and running falls;
at seventy-seven, dread for ruined knees.
Fetal curl. Afraid to move. —Can you get up?—No.
DeWitt, it's Kimmy, I saw you fall.
Don't move. We've called an ambulance.

※ ※ ※

Kimberley Grey. On the flight from Denver
to Portland, she had settled
in the row behind me trading life stories with
an older woman seat-mate.
I'm a poet, she'd announced.
I'm going to a writers' convention.
I'm a triplet. I hate my mother.
She earned $1000 by giving up her scheduled seat;
slept in the airport, boarded this flight.
The older woman admitted she had two boys,
and since this younger woman was a writer
recommended a bestselling romance.
Both were talking to themselves, I thought,
not to each other. I shut my eyes.

※ ※ ※

As we filed out to the gate
pulling our rolling suitcases,
I turned and spoke to the Poet, who
was blonde, pleasant looking and
worldly enough to credit
good intentions: "I overheard
you're going to AWP." I had directions to
the MAX Red Line trolley, direct to City Center,
cheaper than Uber or shuttle. We could
find our way together. She agreed.
We chatted as we rode, discovering connections.

She had been a Stanford Fellow.
She knew poet and memoirist John Evans,
who taught at Stanford, and
whose books I had reviewed.

I'd co-founded *Ploughshares* before she was born,
and had served on the AWP Board decades ago.
She was chairing a panel Friday
about teaching empathy.

As we both checked in at the downtown Hilton,
we wished each other well.

❦ ❦ ❦

I spent my jet-lagged afternoon
wandering through the book-fair,
a mile's walk from the hotel. Each
convention was deja vu:
Denver, Miami, Philadelphia,
Tucson, Tampa, Atlanta, Chicago, New York,
Washington DC, Boston.
Annual attendances had swelled
to 25,000 in recent years, the book fair
to 500 exhibitors, and concurrent panels
to hundreds. I'd almost skipped Portland
since my publisher didn't take a table
and my school no longer covered the trip.

But vanity prevailed. I'd stay two nights;
depart for Boston late Saturday.

🌺 🌺 🌺

I'd never ask, but Kimmy
(I remembered her name)
instantly grasped my plight.
To her, I was a compatriot.
EMTs arrived, got me onto a stretcher,
lifted me into the ambulance.
Both knees felt dislocated or broken.
I couldn't support weight.
Kimmy climbed in behind me,
bringing my shoulder bag and cap.

The EMTs asked my choice, one hospital
a half-mile away or another a mile; I chose
the nearest, which turned out to be
the Oregon Health and Science University Hospital
and renowned (I would discover) for orthopedics.
Was my running life over? How to reach my wife?
The ambulance slowed, bumped, and turned
with emergency whoops,
I glimpsed a blur of pines out the back.
Then we arrived. They rolled me in,
lifted me onto a bed. EMTs left.
I had my insurance card in my bag.
Kimmy took charge, got me signed in.

I thanked and urged her to leave,
but she refused. I needed an advocate.
(Later I learned she'd switched
from nursing to poetry in college.)

I hadn't begun to process
the complications. My wife Connie
was at work and about to leave for
a math teacher's convention in San Diego.

After a sonar scan of both knees,
then x-rays and consultations, the diagnosis:
"Bilateral complete quad tendon rupture.
Extension mechanism not intact. Repair
within week in Boston or Portland."

⁕ ⁕ ⁕

I was helpless. Couldn't travel
with legs immobilized, no matter
how sedated. By luck their
top surgeon was available tomorrow.

Connie and I spoke on my cell;
she also spoke to the doctor, and
we agreed to the operation.
She'd fly out and get a B&B
as soon as she could.

Once admitted, I was moved
to a private room, where
Kimmy and I chatted about poetry.
Her first collection had won a prize
from Persea. I mentioned that
I had a new poem in *On the Seawall,* and .
she not only knew the editor, but served
as assistant editor. More synchronicity!

She looked up my poem on her phone,
and liked it (she said). I gave her
one of my books from the shoulder bag.
I had a signing tomorrow
at the *Solstice* table; could she tell
them to cancel? Also tell the hotel
to cancel my room, and have them
pack my belongings and
store them? I'd left some books,
electric razor and toothbrush,
some clothes in drawers.

She left for her panel at noon.
Not to worry. She'd be back at four.

Meanwhile, I was rolled
to an examination room, where
the surgeon, Dr. Jacqueline Brady,
a woman in her thirties and just a week
back from having her first baby,
asked my story again:
a writer and long-time runner

from Boston who fell off a curb
on his way to a convention, etc.

They would suture my tendons
and reattach them to my patellas.
I looked in good condition;
I should be able to fly home
after a few weeks in rehab.

I called her "The Bee's Knees."
Mentioned that my brother
had been a cancer surgeon
who insisted on carving
our Thanksgiving turkey.

She took notes and signed forms,
then moved on. They'd operate
first thing tomorrow.

Back in my room: Kimmy returned.
The panel had gone well; she'd
told my friends at the book fair
and gathered signatures on
a get-well card. My books
had sold out at the *Solstice* table.
She'd brought my suitcase.

We made a list of blessings
and curses. *Grateful for*:
friends and generous strangers,
medical coverage, emergency service,

first-rate hospital, docs and staff,
for injury not being worse
for hotel room refund,
for canceling return flight,
for cell phone messaging,
for Kimmy's problem solving.
Curses included the accident,
my stupid choice in coming at all,
bad luck, lasting damage,
legs I can't lift, to sit or walk,
missing not only a book signing here,
but four others coming in May,
and forcing Connie to make the trip
and upsetting plans for
her convention and later
for trips to Miami to be with
her dying sister, and to Hoboken,
to help our son and his wife
with birth of their first child.

Kimmy asked me to text her
just before they took me in;
so she could time her visit
and say goodbye.
Her own plane left on Sunday,
when Connie would arrive.

Orderlies came at dawn, rolled me
out to elevator, then
more corridors and turns,
through swinging doors into

bright lights overhead, doctors'
faces masked (I made out
Dr. Brady's, who said "Good morning");
all wearing gloves, caps and tunics,
I was lifted and slid onto the operating
table, pillows under knees. The anesthetist
cupped mouth and nose: "Count out-loud to ten."

I woke in my room. Whatever was,
was over. On my back, I was raised up,
knees bandaged, and bent at 30 degrees
in thigh-to-ankle braces, with lower legs
resting on foam supports. As long as
I didn't move, pain kept at bay.
A circulation sleeve squeezed regularly.

Tom, my middle-aged floor
nurse introduced himself by
telling jokes as if rehearsing
for a stand-up act. I winced
and smirked along to be polite.

❧ ❧ ❧

Dr. Brady stopped in later
and explained the operation. My
tendons were like spaghetti, she said.
With each knee, she gathered strings
into two strands, and threaded each
through a separate tunnel drilled through

the kneecap, then tied them together.
Mechanically my legs could bear
weight again, but the tendons had
to heal and muscles strengthen.
A PT person would visit later
to start exercises. They'd keep the
braces at 0-30 degree range
for six weeks, then gradually increase.
Full recovery could take from
six months to two years,
but I should be able to walk,
bike, swim, and even jog again,
depending on how hard I worked.

I told her about my writer friend
Andre Dubus, an ex-Marine,
who had stopped to help
motorists on a late-night highway,
been hit himself, and lost both legs;
how he'd lived in pain, but
written essays about his disability.

She asked about my book
which I described as meditations
on key words such as
conscience, voice, and privilege,
and gave her a copy, signed
to "Bee's Knees" with thanks.

Her assistant stopped in later
to change my dressings—loosening

the braces and giving
me first glimpse of each long
scar and swollen row of stitches.

Next the PT woman arrived.
Told me: "Sit up, take my hands.
Surgeon says you're good
to hold your weight." She and
her helper held my legs
in their braces. I couldn't bend yet.
"Keep going," she urged.
  As I sat and pushed, they dragged
  me to sit over the bed edge,
  lower my legs. Feeling dizzy,
  "I'm going to black out," I said.
  And did. Was looking up
  at PT's troubled face,
  framed in her burka.
"Did I black out?" "Yes," she said.
"We try again later."

  I was flattered that Kimmy
  brought her roommate to meet me:
  Chi Elliot, from Stanford.
  They'd been on the panel together.

  I filled in Kimmy about the surgery.
  We chatted together about books
  and lives; wished each other well
  and vowed to keep in touch.

(From back home, she posted
her perspective on facebook:
how she'd been honored to moderate
a panel on empathy and inclusion; how
she'd spent much of her time at
the hospital "with a wonderful writer"
whose accident she had witnessed;
and how "This is the real human work,
this being there and helping each other
in this otherwise difficult world.")

Thanks to her, word of my accident
spread quickly from the Book Fair
to colleagues and friends back East.
John Skoyles was first to call, as he'd
been first to encourage my essays
and poems. He had a new book from the
same publisher; and we had hoped to read
together at AWP, but then he'd decided
to stay home. A friend in San Francisco
heard and emailed, offering to drive up.
Lee Hope, editor of *Solstice* called,
was there anything she could do?
A friend of Connie's, an artist in Boston,
who previously had been a Portland
hospital orderly, seriously considered
driving cross-country in a van to retrieve me.

Connie arrived Sunday afternoon,
having settled in a nearby B&B.
My loving, resourceful partner,
she splendidly took charge.

She met Dr. Brady, Ted the Nurse,
and the hospital's social worker.
She'd also brought my laptop.
She was prepared to stay
until I healed enough to fly home.
We'd worry about money later.

I'd grown used to hospital routines.
My three-day constipation from pain meds
was resolved in comical fashion
while Connie visited. Tom had given me
a prune-juice cocktail and as
I started to cramp, velcro-ed me
into an power-sling attached
to overhead tracks; lifted
and swung me bare-assed in
my gown until I hovered over
a waiting commode;
then shouted "Brown Alert!"
which left us all laughing.

The same apparatus swung me
to sit in a reclining chair.
I learned to "scootch" on a board
from bed to wheelchair. And Connie
pushed me for a tour of corridors
hung with modern paintings
(some doctor had been a major collector),
and out to a terrace for fresh air, where
we watched a glassed-in gondola
ride up and down the mountain.

I'd come to know the night nurses.
A twenty-something single father, Sam.
who became companion to my insomnia
and was eager to study good fiction.
He loved Hemingway and raved about
H.P. Lovecraft, whom I had barely read.

Dr. Brady, having read my essays,
recommended a new word for me
to consider: "Resilience." Yes, I'd said,
and thanked her. I'd been moved
by a Youtube journal of man
with my injury on one side only,
who'd healed in stages over eleven weeks.
then ended with his first jogging.

The hospital needed my room and
the social worker had discovered an opening
at one of the best rehabs,
"The Pearl," on Lake Oswego.
She arranged for my discharge
and insurance okays and
I was transported in a wheelchair
van with Connie next morning.

Thus began next stop in my journey,
For nine more days, I continued:
medicated, bedridden and dependent.
The attendants were overtaxed
by needier, more elderly patients,
whose cries and groans I heard

through walls. A single doctor
was on call. Head nurses and PTs
were professional, but most
of the attendants were trainees
yet to start nursing school.

Connie took walks each morning,
then Uber-ed to join me each afternoon.
She brought me family news.
She'd hoped we could leave
in a matter of days, but after conferring
with the PTs and doctor, realized
that I'd need another week at least.
I told her to go alone, then come back
when I was ready, but she refused.

I could lever into a wheelchair.
I'd been able to stand. In PT gym
I took first steps, having heaved
myself up between parallel bars
with hands and arms taking my weight;
then lowered myself back
into my wheelchair. I thought of
our children's baby steps.
Each day's practice left me spent.

I showered in the wheelchair with
trash bags wrapped around braces.
Melatonin helped me sleep, despite
the goat cries of a distant patient:

"Water, please…Hurry up…Help….help….
Right now…right now…Where are we?"
Otherwise my mind whirred.
I read and worked on poems.

To fly home I needed to master
wheelchair and walker; stand,
turn, take steps, and lower myself
to sit, while someone lifted my legs.
The PT put me through a simulation.

Connie and Pearl's social worker
called the airlines. Alaska Air offered
35 inches leg room and a removable
armrest in a first row seat before
their bulkhead—for a premium.
Connie made our reservation.
The social worker booked me
into a Cambridge rehab and arranged
for medical transit to Portland's airport
and pick-up at Logan. The Pearl
had gifted me its wheelchair.

The six-hour flight was torture.
Even with shoes off to gain another
inch, I had to unlock the braces
and jam myself diagonally, feet pushing
against the bulkhead and crowding Connie.
Finally, we landed. Terra cognita.
I felt oriented again, or almost.
We deplaned, found my chair, our bags,

found the ambulance waiting, and
headed west along the river
to Neville Center at Fresh Pond.

My roommate, Peter Bloom,
was younger but in agony.
His knee implant had become infected,
then replaced by another, again infected.
Drugs dulled his pain, but
unless his antibiotics worked,
he would need an amputation.
Every few hours at night
his IV alarm sounded, until
a nurse brought a fresh pouch.
Incessant TV helped distract him.
We traded stories. He was an engineer,
I think, educated, divorced. No kids.
He had a brother who visited,
and argued on the phone
about an inheritance.
Peter tried to be sociable
and envied my progress and family.

I practiced with a walker now,
push-sliding on my own
to the bathroom, unlike him. I
made long trips up and down
the halls by myself. Soon I'd be discharged.
We rehearsed a car transfer,

and when the time came
(Good Friday and Passover),
I left with Connie, wheelchair,
walker, laptop, clothes, and meds,
wished Peter farewell, and
easily fit into our backseat,
back to one door, feet to other.

Our brief drive home was euphoric.
Our daughter and son-in-law met
us in the driveway and lifted me
in tilted wheelchair up one steep step
then over the sill of our back door.

We heard that night that our son's,
first child, Olivia, had been born.
Mother and baby were fine.
Dave's in-laws were near them, but
we were torn with yearning.

🌺 🌺 🌺

Connie had rearranged the house.
From upstairs guest room,
she had slid down the queen-sized
bed and frame to the living-room.
Had shoved the couch against
the fireplace and mantel, bed's
head against back wall with foot
towards picture window opposite,
front door and staircase to the left.

Bathroom was around the corner,
my study to left, kitchen to right,
and through the kitchen, down one step
to TV room, the backdoor.

Our home PT suggested stacking
flagstones to make each step
more gradual for crutches;
and my first time in and out
would be another milestone.

I learned to sleep on my side,
supporting one brace with the other.
I saw my health plan's orthopedist,
who increased my bending range.
I practiced leg lifts, foot lifts,
seated marching. Pushing forward
to stand was too much. I had a booster
toilet seat, and with Connie's help,
slid over tub's flat rim to tub chair,
and showered with braces covered.

The one reading that I hadn't cancelled
was in Harvard Square. Connie drove me
and I read from my wheelchair,
blessed to see friends, sell ten copies,
and leave ten more on consignment.

Our son and family drove up to visit.
We—I—got to hold the baby at last.

I managed well enough at home
(with our daughter nearby on call)
that Connie left for a week
with her sister, Lonne, in Miami;
she returned, then left again as
Lonne went into hospice and passed.
I flew down with our daughter
for the memorial service. Though
awkward and cautious with only
knee braces, I sat, climbed stairs,
and even took them off to swim.
I did my best to join Connie
in joy and in grief.

The orthopedist declared me healed,
though I needed to keep strengthening.
We moved the bed back upstairs.

By Labor Day, I had full use of the house.
I wrote in my study. I could drive alone.
I had more local readings. I had
another book of essays coming out.
In October, we drove to Kutztown, PA,
where I had a University reading overnight,
and then to Wayne, my home town, for
my 60th high school reunion and
a bookstore reading for classmates.

Connie retired from Boston Public Schools,
then continued consulting.
I finished my first book of poems.

We helped our daughter buy
a house up the street.

Concerns about Covid shrank
attendance for 2020's AWP
in San Antonio, while the 2021
convention would be only virtual—
not that I'd consider going again.

I read Kimberly Grey's next collection,
systems for the future of feeling,
in fall 2020, with its dedication
"to myself and strangers"; and was
impressed by her riddling,
lived poems about language, love,
marriage, grief, and negative
capability; her surprising forms;
and intertextual "interviews"
with such wights as Gertrude Stein,
Ann Carson, Jack Gilbert, Sina Quryas
(whom I'd never heard of).
and Ludwig Wittenstein
(heard of, but never read).
I visited her virtual bookstore
launch. Someday, I hope,
we'll get a chance to read together.

BEAUTIFUL FLOWER

1

Here is Evan Fraser, Amherst sophomore, dreaming of a just society. Son of an English professor at the University of Northern Florida. Came to Amherst on a merit scholarship. He wrote his high school English teacher that he sought with his life to express a brilliance that would stun the eye, so the image would linger. Five feet, six inches, 140 pounds, white male, reads the Town of Amherst Police report. No evidence of drug use. Interviews with students, teachers, and neighbors determined that he was a "normal young man," "decent," "earnest student," "good sense of humor." He lived in an apartment off campus, where residents saw him working hard, riding his motorcycle. He was survived by an older brother and sister. Mother died when he was fifteen. Father baffled. The message, the letter left for friends, society, the world: "I am Socrates, Jesus, Gandhi. Love one another."

2

Long run first, perhaps. Wonder at this world, this envelope. The shower, scalding, then cold. Skin glows. Shaves. The layered, cotton clothing in 80-degree heat. Save the Whales T-shirt. Heavy socks. The five-gallon can, full and sloshing. The rehearsals and viewings of news clips over and over. Saturate grass first. Heave can over head, after clothes have been soaked. Sting in eyes, bitter on lips, fumes, cough, breathe deep. Quick, before anyone realizes or interferes. Intensity of purpose, graceful, efficiency of movement. Like ablution. Flick the Bic.

3

Sears like hunger, rape, birth, bursting bones, like impotence before earthquake or tidal wave, like cancer at its worst, like killing cramps, migraine, jaws, tightening, tightening. The pain is other, tangible, enemy and lover, engrossing, intimate. A corridor. A tunnel that I shoulder through, breathless and gasping. But then sheer vision, faith.

4

Recorded lifetimes, stop-time photos, sped up after 90 years, so that faces morph like unfurling, then withering flowers. The immolator, one of this study, needs to be slowed down in order to match the rhythm; his 19 years ending in the stop frame, now, of two minutes, slow motioning his lighting of the bic, the flame like a bud, a flower unfurling, and then the bloom slowly wrapping him like a silken, bright robe, or even garlands blooming, something fragile, fragrant and soft, his face dissolving, as others melt at other speeds, within the liquidity, the pouring and the light.

5

He stands before his 15th annual class in Shakespearian Tragedy. "Liebentot," he says to the 13 faces, bright, young faces, college juniors, though sleepy and hung over this Tuesday, "dying for love. How do we understand this? Tristan and Isolde? Dido for Anaeus? Romeo for Juliet (the dope); Juliet for Romeo? Othello for Desdemona? Anthony for Cleopatra, and then a whole act later, Cleopatra, with the asp sucking its mistress asleep? What is this? Jonestown?"

You, Ms. Bright one, Ms. Mystery, YOU say: "Not Jonestown. Just proof. Proof of eternal devotion. Most lovers die one day at a time, like alcoholics stay sober. The silver, the golden anniversary. There's our proof, whatever they may think they mean themselves; they mean what they do. The deed in living, like those gison statues that Leonard Baskin did on the Smith College campus. Let attention be paid. Not kings and princes, memorialized for nobility on burial caskets. But a steelworker, a miner... beer belly distended, naked, noble too in his self sacrifice, his daily endurance, his lifetime's love—" or perhaps, you sneer, "his failure of imagination." I wait and you go on. "One day at a time, like an alcoholic staying sober. Down all the days, adding up. A marriage, a career, a life's meaning. For the tragic characters, that's all sped up, is all. Same passion, less time."

"An animal in its individual development passes through a series of constructive stages like those in the evolutionary development of the race to which it belongs…," states Haaeckel's biogenic law from 1868.

Primordial soup. Thick and slab. Fire burn, and cauldron bubble. Blake: "Eternity rolled wide apart/wide asunder rolling." Complex protein. Protozoa, 4 billion years ago. Sperm swarm, tail churn. Nature's germains. The single penetration, egg ignites. DNA. Chromosomes. Cells divide, divide. Germinal to embryonic. 3 billion years, future in the instant. Cambrian is gill arches. Placenta sea. My mother is a fish. Blake: "The globe of life blood trembled / Branching out into roots / Fibrous, writhing upon the winds." Now inner ear and neck, cartilages of larynx. Tail emerges, disappears. Zygote into embryo. Ordovician. 400 million years. 3rd moon, cartilage to bone. 4th moon, heart forms; 5th moon, ears, eyes, arms, and legs. Embryo to fetus. Mesozoic. Jurassic. 200 million years ago. 6th moon, early primates. Skeleton visible. Sex organs distinct. Translucent skin. Eyelashes. Eyebrows. Body movements. 7th moon, survival outside womb probable. Pleistocene. Homo erectus. Neanderthal. 100 thousand years ago. Holocene. Weight gains. Increased activity in kidneys, heart. 9th moon, fetus to newborn. You. Me.

9

I ask you, now? The miracle, the life. The person out of the person, body from body, flesh from flesh, crying we come forth. Time itself, apocalypse; ignition; Adam to atom; all existence in the flash.

10

King Nebuchadnezzsar cast Shadrack, Meshach, and Abednego into the burning fiery furnace but this was showmanship, the clincher, preserving flesh from fire: "the hair of their heads was not singed, their mantles were not harmed, and no smell of fire had come upon them." Then there is purgatory, holy fires cleansing to essence. "I lean forward over my clasped hands and stare into the fire," says Dante, "thinking of human bodies I once saw burned, and once more see them there."

To imagine burning is not to burn.

CORPUS

A life's work left behind;
remains preserved
(even if in progress),
to be considered as a whole.
Usually already public,
but sometimes not.

Legacy, canon, ouvre,
as brief as single book,
or daunting as many.
Not to be confused
with "papers" or archives.

Corporal punishment,
i.e. damaging the corpus,
physically or critically.
Book burning? Censorship?
Cultural agendas? Defamation?

Sir Philip Sydney defined
poetry as "that which
we will not willingly let die,"
He incorporates humanity,
despite our fears of evolution/devolution,
and Tennyson's "anxiety of language."

Corpse, carcass, or cadaver,
we call the dead ones.
Ashes if cremains.
Or mummy if preserved;
or cryogenics' frozen sleeper;
or zombie, if still walking.

Aesthetes fight the tyrannies
of hunger, pain and lust. Hedonists
and epicures glorify life's touch,
seizing their days, while addicts
crave chemical states.

Carnival or Lent? Fast or feast?
Corpulent or lean?
Celibate or celebrate?
Bonfire of the vanities?

Poet Thomas Lux,
suffering from cancer,
wrote a parting litany
like *Good Night, Moon's:*
" ...let us praise the joy-bringer
for these seven things: 1) right lung,
2) left lung, 3) heart, 4) left brain,
5) right brain, 6) tongue,
7) the body to put them in.
Thank you, joy-bringer!"

Our body's worth
about a dollar for elements.
However, half a million
for organs freshly harvested.

Donated to science,
it serves to keep on giving.

For the familiar allegory
of body politic, see *Coriolanus:*
"all the body's members"
rebelled "against the belly."

Heroes show battle scars.
Would-be saints mortify flesh.
Self-lash, wear hair shirts
and sleep in coffins.

Others dream of heaven,
where each soul is dressed
again in youthful best.

Or of re-incarnation
up and down great being's chain.

"My body to you," says
both lover and writer,
person and works;
embodied and dis-,
fleshed out and transmogrified.

Acknowledgments

"Shofar" in *The Woven Tale Press*: December, 2024

"Corpus" in *Constellations*, Winter 2024;

"Beautiful Flower" in *Pensive*, Winter 2024.

Thanks to these magazines and their editors.

DeWitt Henry

DeWitt Henry

Born in Wayne, PA. Radnor High School, 1959; A.B. Amherst College, 1963; M.A. in English, Harvard University, 1965; Ph.D. English, Harvard University, 1971; completed requirements for M.F.A. University of Iowa, 1968 (did not take the degree).

Founding editor of *Ploughshares* literary magazine, and active editor and director 1971-1995. Interim Director of *Ploughshares* 6/2007-10/2008. Professor Emeritus, Emerson College, 2016-present. Professor, Writing, Literature, and Publishing, Emerson College, 2006-2015; Associate Professor 1989 to 2006: hired as Assistant Professor 1983; Acting Chairperson 1987-8; Chairperson 1989-93.

DeWitt is also a contributing editor to *Solstice: A Magazine of Diverse Voices* (2013-) and to *The Woven Tale Press: Arts and Literary Journal* (2016-).

Also by DeWitt Henry

Fiction

Top Cop Kills
Pierian Springs Press, Spring 2025

THE MARRIAGE OF ANNA MAYE POTTS
New Edition with Foreword by Margot Livesey
Pierian Springs Press, Spring 2024
1ˢᵗ Edition, University of Tennessee Press, 2001
(Winner of the **Peter Taylor Prize for the Novel**)

FALLING: SIX STORIES
CreateSpace, 2016

Essays

SWEET MARJORAM: NOTES AND ESSAYS
Plume Editions / MadHat Press, 2018

Memoir

ENDINGS & BEGINNINGS: FAMILY ESSAYS
MadHat Press, 2021
(Long-listed for the **PEN/Diamonstein-Spielvogel Award**
for the Art of the Essay, 2022)

VISIONS OF A WAYNE CHILDHOOD
CreateSpace, 2012

SWEET DREAMS: A FAMILY HISTORY
Hidden River Press, 2011

SAFE SUICIDE: ESSAYS, NARRATIVES, AND MEDITATIONS
Red Hen Press, 2008

Poetry

Do I Dream Or Wake?
Pierian Springs Press, December 2024

TRIM RECKONINGS: POEMS
Pierian Springs Press, November 2023

FOUNDLINGS: FOUND POEMS FROM PROSE
New Edition with Notes, Sources & Full Color Artwork
Pierian Springs Press, October 2023

RESTLESS FOR WORDS: POEMS
Finishing Line Press, February 2023

FOUNDLINGS: FOUND POEMS FROM PROSE
Life Before Man/Gazebo Books, May 2022

Anthologies

SORROW'S COMPANY: WRITERS ON LOSS AND GRIEF
Beacon Press, 2001

BREAKING INTO PRINT: EARLY STORIES AND INSIGHTS INTO GETTING PUBLISHED; A PLOUGHSHARES ANTHOLOGY
Beacon Press, 2000

FATHERING DAUGHTERS: REFLECTIONS BY MEN
(with James Alan McPherson)
Beacon Press 1998, pb. 1999

OTHER SIDES OF SILENCE: NEW FICTION FROM PLOUGHSHARES
Faber and Faber, 1993, o.p.

THE PLOUGHSHARES READER: NEW FICTION FOR THE 80s
(Winner **Third Annual Editors Book Award**)
Pushcart Press, 1984, NAL, 1985

www.ingramcontent.com/pod-product-compliance
Lightning Source LLC
Chambersburg PA
CBHW030529130626
46549CB00007B/3172